Contents

Some words are shown in bold, **like this**. They are explained in the glossary on page 23.

What is a circle?

A circle is a **flat**, round shape.

You can see flat shapes but you cannot pick them up.

Finding Shapes

Circles

Diyan Leake

www.raintreepublishers.co.uk
Visit our website to find out more information about **Raintree** books.

To order:
☎ Phone 44 (0) 1865 888112
▤ Send a fax to 44 (0) 1865 314091
▣ Visit the Raintree Bookshop at **www.raintreepublishers.co.uk** to browse our catalogue and order online.

First published in Great Britain by Raintree, Halley Court, Jordan Hill, Oxford OX2 8EJ, part of Harcourt Education.
Raintree is a registered trademark of Harcourt Education Ltd.

© Harcourt Education Ltd 2006
First published in paperback in 2007
The moral right of the proprietor has been asserted.

Editorial: Diyan Leake
Design: Joanna Hinton-Malivoire
Illustration: Darren Lingard
Picture research: Maria Joannou
Production: Victoria Fitzgerald
Originated by Dot Gradations Ltd
Printed and bound in China by South China Printing Company

10 digit ISBN 1 844 21331 5 (HB)
13 digit ISBN 978 1844 21331 3 (HB)
10 09 08 07 06
10 9 8 7 6 5 4 3 2 1

10 digit ISBN 1 844 21336 6 (PB)
13 digit ISBN 978 1844 21336 8 (PB)
10 09 08 07
10 9 8 7 6 5 4 3 2 1

British Library Cataloguing in Publication Data
Leake, Diyan
516.1'5
Finding Shapes: Circles
A full catalogue record for this book is available from the British Library.

Acknowledgements
The publishers would like to thank the following for permission to reproduces photographs: Alamy Images pp. **5**, **14** (Alex Segre), **15** (Andre Jenny), back cover (traffic lights, Alex Segre); Corbis p. **13** (Paul A. Souders), back cover (moon, Paul A. Souders); Harcourt Education Ltd pp. **6** (Malcolm Harris), **7** (Malcolm Harris), **8** (Malcolm Harris), **9** (Malcolm Harris), **10** (Malcolm Harris), **11** (Malcolm Harris), **12** (Malcolm Harris), **17** (Malcolm Harris), **18** (Malcolm Harris), **19** (Tudor Photography), **20** (Malcolm Harris), **21** (Malcolm Harris), **22** (Tudor Photography), **23** (cylinder, Tudor Photography; hollow, Malcolm Harris)

Cover photograph reproduced with the permission of Corbis

Every effort has been made to contact copyright holders of any material reproduced in this book. Any omissions will be rectified in subsequent printings if notice is given to the publishers.

The author and publisher would like to thank Patti Barber, specialist in Early Years Education, University of London Institute of Education, for her advice and assistance in the preparation of this book.

…ies from

middle

edge

Circles are **curved** all the way round.

They are the same length from the edge to the middle.

Can I see circles at home?

There are lots of circles at home.

Some of them are in the living room.

These mugs and bottles have circles on them.

What other circles are there at home?

There are circles in the kitchen.

Plates and baking tins have a circle shape.

Round fruit and vegetables look like circles when we slice them.

Can I see circles at school?

There are lots of circles at school.

Some circles are big and some circles are small.

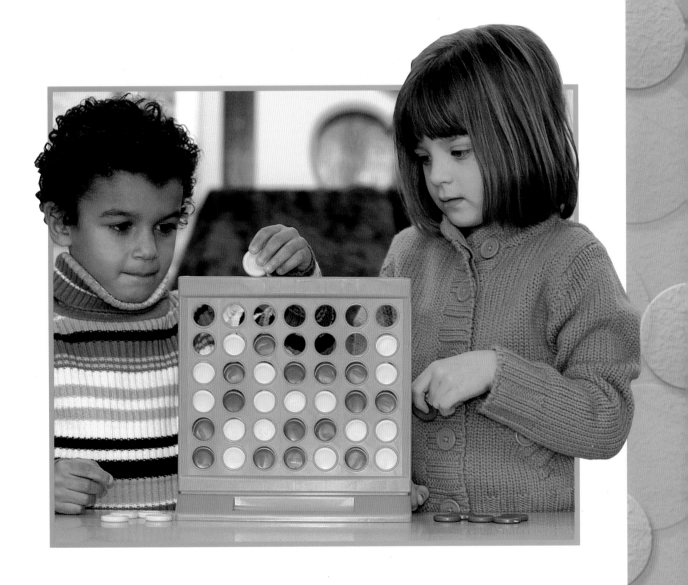

You can see blue circles and yellow circles in this game.

Are there circles outside?

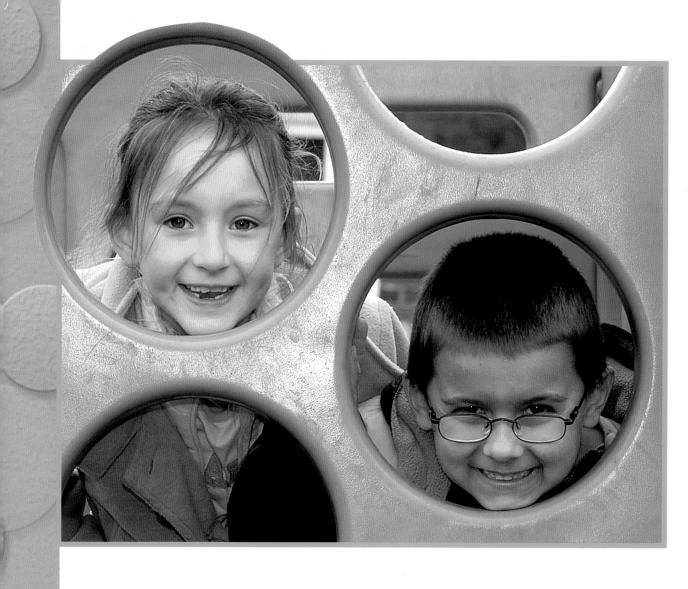

This climbing frame is outside.

You can look through the circles on it.

The full moon is a circle in the sky.

The night sky is not so dark when the moon is full.

Are there circles in town?

We can see all sorts of circles in town.

We see a red, yellow, or green circle when we look at traffic lights.

Some buildings have circles
on them.

The clock face on this church
is a circle.

Can circles be part of other shapes?

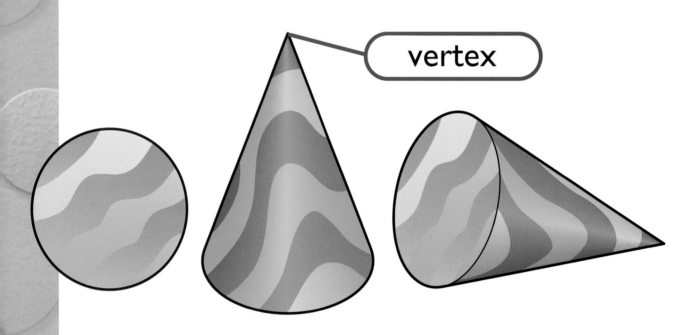

vertex

A **cone** has a circle at one end and a **vertex** at the other.

The vertex is the pointed part of the cone.

These cones are **hollow** so you can put ice cream in them.

What other cones can you find at a party?

These party hats are **cones**.

Cones do not roll if you put them on their **flat** side.

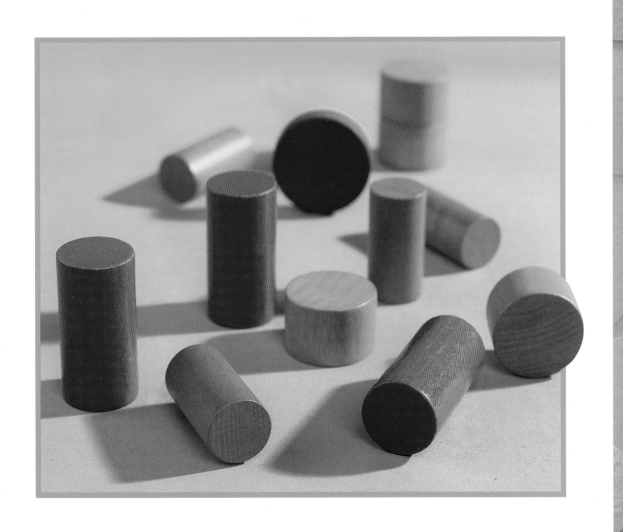

A **cylinder** has a circle at each end.

Cylinders can be big or small.

Where can I find cylinders?

There are lots of **cylinders** in the kitchen.

These cylinders are shiny.

Cylinders do not roll when they stand on their ends.

They can roll when they are on their side.

Can I go on a circle hunt?

Walk around the room and see how many circles you can find!

Glossary

cone
shape that has a circle at one end and a pointed vertex at the other

curved
not straight

cylinder
shape that has a circle at each end and a curved face in between

flat
has no thickness to it

hollow
has space inside

vertex
corner of a shape

Index

Note to parents and teachers

Reading non-fiction texts for information is an important part of a child's literacy development. Readers can be encouraged to ask simple questions and then use the text to find the answers. Each chapter in this book begins with a question. Read the questions together. Look at the pictures. Talk about what the answer might be. Then read the text to find out if your predictions were correct. To develop readers' enquiry skills, encourage them to think of other questions they might ask about the topic. Discuss where you could find the answers. Assist children in using the contents page, picture glossary, and index to practise research skills and new vocabulary.